A Simple Prayer Book

All booklets are published thanks to the generous support of the members of the Catholic Truth Society

CATHOLIC TRUTH SOCIETY
PUBLISHERS TO THE HOLY SEE

Contents

Let us go forward in hope! 3
Usual prayers 5
Morning prayers 9
Night prayers 10
Additional prayers 11
Litany of the Blessed Virgin 18
Preparing for Confession 21
Sacrament of Penance 26
Prayers for Holy Communion 28
Benediction 34
The way of the Cross 38
The Holy Rosary 41
A quarter of an hour before
the Blessed Sacrament 44
Summary of Christian Doctrine 48
Marriage and the Church 55
Fasting and abstinence 56
Holy Mass 57
The order of Mass 60

Imprimatur: Ralph Brown VG, Westminster. The English text of The Order of Mass has been approved by the Hierarchies of England and Wales, of Scotland, and of Ireland. English translation Copyright © 1969 and 1971 International Committee on English in the Liturgy, Inc. All rights reserved.

– ❧ Let us go forward in Hope! ❧ –

His Holiness, Pope John Paul II

A new millennium is opening before the Church like a vast ocean upon which we shall venture, relying on the help of Christ. The Son of God, who became incarnate two thousand years ago out of love for humanity, is at work even today: we need discerning eyes to see this and, above all, a generous heart to become the instruments of his work... Now, the Christ whom we have contemplated and loved bids us to set out once more on our journey: "Go therefore and make disciples out of all nations, baptising in the name of the Father, and of the Son and of the Holy Spirit." *(Mt 28:19) (John Paul II, Novo Millennio Ineunte)*

— ❧ Why do you seek me Lord ? ❧ —

In the Incarnation God himself speaks to me. By becoming one of us in history, Christ fully reveals man to man himself and makes his supreme calling clear by revealing the mystery of the Father's love. It is here Christianity differs from all other religions through which man has long searched for his God. It is God who comes in person to speak to me of himself and show me the path by which He may be reached.

Christ incarnate is the fulfilment of the yearning present in all the religions of all mankind! It is the mystery of grace. In Christ religion is no longer a blind search for God, but the response of faith to God who reveals himself to me. I can speak to God as my Creator and Father. So God not only speaks to me but seeks me out! The Incarnation attests that God has gone in search of me, because he loves me eternally and wishes to raise me in Christ to the dignity of an adoptive son. Why do you search for me as a special possession unlike any other creature!

I turned away from you, I allowed myself to be led astray by the enemy, Satan, who persuaded me that I too was God, capable of knowing good and evil, making the world according to my own will without reference to the divine will. How you have searched for me! Wanting me to abandon the path of evil that I have taken, to overcome the evil which is found in human history. Overcoming evil: this is the meaning of the Redemption. My Redemption!

(Adapted from *Tertio Millennio Adveniente* John Paul II)

❧ Usual Prayers ❧

Our Father

Our Father, who art in heaven, hallowed be thy name. Thy Kingdom come. Thy will be done on earth as it is in heaven. Give us this day our daily bread, and forgive us our trespasses, as we forgive those who trespass against us. And lead us not into temptation, but deliver us from evil. Amen.

Hail Mary

Hail, Mary, full of grace, the Lord is with thee: blessed art thou among women, and blessed is the fruit of thy womb, Jesus. Holy Mary, Mother of God, pray for us sinners, now, and at the hour of our death. Amen.

Glory be to the Father

Glory be to the Father, and to the Son, and to the Holy Spirit. As it was in the beginning, is now, and ever shall be, world without end. Amen.

I Believe (The Apostles' Creed)

I believe in God, the Father almighty, creator of heaven and earth. I believe in Jesus Christ, his only Son, our Lord. He was conceived by the power of the Holy Spirit and born of the Virgin Mary. He suffered under Pontius Pilate, was crucified, died, and was buried. He descended to the dead. On the third day he rose again. He ascended into heaven, and is seated at the right hand of the Father. He will come again to judge the living and the dead. I believe in the Holy Spirit, the holy Catholic Church, the communion of saints, the forgiveness of sins, the resurrection of the body, and the life everlasting. Amen.

The Confiteor

I confess to almighty God that I have sinned through my own fault, in my thoughts and in my words, in what I have done, and in what I have failed to do; and I ask blessed Mary, ever virgin, and all the angels and saints, to pray for me to the Lord our God.

An Act of Contrition

O my God, because you are so good, I am very sorry that I have sinned against you and by the help of your grace I will not sin again.

The Memorare

Remember, O most loving Virgin Mary, that it is a thing unheard of, that anyone ever had recourse to your protection, implored your help, or sought your intercession, and was left forsaken. Filled therefore with confidence in your goodness I fly to you, O Mother, Virgin of virgins. To you I come, before you I stand, a sorrowful sinner. Despise not my poor words, O Mother of the Word of God, but graciously hear and grant my prayer.

The Angelus

May be said morning, noon, and night, to put us in mind that God the Son became man for our salvation.

V. The Angel of the Lord declared to Mary:
R. And she conceived of the Holy Spirit.
   Hail Mary...

V. Behold the handmaid of the Lord:
R. Be it done to me according to your word.
   Hail Mary...

V. And the Word was made Flesh:
R. And dwelt among us.
   Hail Mary...

V. Pray for us, O holy Mother of God.
R. That we may be made worthy of the promises of Christ.
   Let us pray:
Pour forth, we beseech you, O Lord, your grace into our hearts, that we, to whom the Incarnation of Christ, your Son, was made known by the message of an angel, may by his passion and cross ✠ be brought to the glory of his resurrection, through the same Christ our Lord. **R.** Amen.
May the divine assistance remain always with us ✠ and may the souls of the faithful departed, through the mercy of God, rest in peace. **R.** Amen.

The Regina Cæli

O Queen of heaven, rejoice! Alleluia.
For he whom you did merit to bear, Alleluia,
Has risen as he said. Alleluia.
Pray for us to God. Alleluia.

V. Rejoice and be glad, O Virgin Mary, Alleluia,
R. For the Lord has risen indeed, Alleluia.

Let us pray:
God our Father, you give joy to the world by the resurrection of your Son, our Lord Jesus Christ. Through the prayers of his mother, the Virgin Mary, bring us to the happiness of eternal life. We ask this through our Lord Jesus Christ, your Son, who lives and reigns with you and the Holy Spirit, one God, for ever and ever. **R.** Amen.

The Hail Holy Queen

Hail, holy Queen, mother of mercy; hail, our life, our sweetness, and our hope! To you do we cry, poor banished children of Eve; to you do we send up our sighs, mourning and weeping in this vale of tears. Turn then, most gracious advocate, your eyes of mercy towards us; and after this our exile, show to us the blessed fruit of your womb, Jesus. O clement, O loving, O sweet Virgin Mary.

V. Pray for us, O holy Mother of God.
R. That we may be made worthy of the promises of Christ.

✠ MORNING PRAYERS ✠

In the name ✠ of the Father...

Our Father. Hail Mary. Glory be. I Believe.

O my God, I believe in you, because you are Truth itself.

O my God, I hope and trust in you, because of your promises to me.

O my God, I love you above all things, because you are so good yourself; teach me to love you daily more and more.

O my God, I offer you all my thoughts, words, actions, and sufferings; and I beseech you to give me your grace that I may not offend you this day, but may faithfully serve you and do your holy will in all things. I entrust myself completely to your boundless mercy today and always.

Holy Mary, be a mother to me. Angels and Saints of God, pray for me. The Lord ✠ bless us and keep us from all evil and bring us to everlasting life.

✠ May the souls of the faithful departed, through the mercy of God, rest in peace. Amen.

During the day: Frequently remind yourself of the loving God by momentary acts of love. Keep away from what leads to sin. Be obedient. Always tell the truth. Do not steal. Do not let anyone lead you to do anything wrong. God is with you. Be afraid of none but God. If you are tempted to sin, make the sign of the Cross and say, "Lord, save me, or I perish". If you have fallen into sin, say, "My God, I am very sorry that I have sinned against you and by the help of your grace, I will not sin again."

✠ Night Prayers ✠

In the name ✠ of the Father...
Our Father. Hail Mary. Glory be. I Believe.
O my God, I thank you for all the benefits which I have ever received from you, and especially this day. Give me light to see what sins I have committed, and grant me the grace to be truly sorry for them.

Here examine your conscience for the faults you have committed during the day. (See pages 21-25)

O my God, because you are so good, I am very sorry that I have sinned against you and by the help of your grace I will not sin again.

Into your hands, O Lord, I commend my spirit; Lord Jesus, receive my soul.

Holy Mary, be a mother to me.

May our Blessed Lady, St Joseph, and all the Saints, pray for us to our Lord, that we may be preserved this night from sin and all evil. Amen.

O my good Angel, whom God has appointed to be my guardian, watch over me during this night. Angels and Saints of God, pray for me. The Lord ✠ bless us and keep us from evil, and bring us to everlasting life.

✠ May the souls of the faithful departed, through the mercy of God, rest in peace. Amen.

❧ Additional Prayers ❧

Act of Faith

My God, I believe in you and all that your Church teaches, because you have said it, and your word is true.

Act of Hope

My God, I hope in you, for grace and for glory, because of your promises, your mercy and your power.

Act of Charity

My God, because you are so good, I love you with all my heart, and for your sake, I love my neighbour as myself.

An Act of Contrition

O my God, I am sorry and beg pardon for all my sins, and detest them above all things, because they deserve your dreadful punishments, because they have crucified my loving Saviour Jesus Christ, and, most of all, because they offend your infinite goodness; and I firmly resolve, by the help of your grace, never to offend you again, and carefully to avoid the occasions of sin.

Commendation

Jesus, Mary and Joseph, I give you my heart and my soul.
Jesus, Mary and Joseph, assist me in my last agony.
Jesus, Mary and Joseph, may I breathe forth my soul in peace with you.

Act of Resignation

O Lord, my God, whatever manner of death is pleasing to you, with all its anguish, pains and sorrows, I now accept from your hand with a resigned and willing spirit.

(A partial indulgence. A plenary indulgence at the hour of death, if the dying person is properly disposed and has been in the habit of reciting some prayers during his or her lifetime).

Prayer to the Holy Spirit

Come, O Holy Spirit, fill the hearts of your faithful, and enkindle in them the fire of your love.

> **V.** Send forth your Spirit and they shall be created.
> **R.** And you shall renew the face of the earth.
> Let us pray:

O God, who taught the hearts of the faithful by the light of the Holy Spirit, grant that by the gift of the same Spirit we may be always truly wise and ever rejoice in his consolation. Through Christ our Lord. **R.** Amen.

For the Faithful Departed

Out of the depths I cry to you, O Lord,
Lord hear my voice!
O let your ears be attentive to the voice of my pleading.
If you, O Lord, should mark our guilt,
Lord, who would survive?
But with you is found forgiveness:

for this we revere you.
My soul is waiting for the Lord,
I count on his word.
My soul is longing for the Lord
more than watchmen for daybreak.
(Let the watchman count on daybreak
and Israel on the Lord).
Because with the Lord there is mercy
and fullness of redemption,
Israel indeed he will redeem from all its iniquity.

V. Eternal rest grant to them, O Lord.
R. And let perpetual light shine upon them.
V. May they rest in peace.
R. Amen.
V. O Lord, hear my prayer.
R. And let my cry come to you

Let us pray:

O God, the Creator and Redeemer of all the faithful, grant to the souls of your servants departed the remission of all their sins, that through our pious supplication they may obtain that pardon which they have always desired; who live and reign for ever and ever. **R.** Amen.

In Temptation

Lord, save me, or I perish. Keep me close to you by your grace, or I shall sin and fall away from you. Jesus, help me; Mary, help me; my holy Angel, watch over me.

In Trouble

In all things may the most holy, the most just, and the most lovable will of God be done, praised, and exalted above all for ever. Your will be done, O Lord, your will be done. The Lord has given, the Lord has taken away; blessed be the name of the Lord.

In Sickness and Pain

Lord, your will be done; I take this for my sins. I offer up to you my sufferings, together with all that my Saviour has suffered for me; and I beg you, through his sufferings, to have mercy on me. Free me from this illness and pain if you will, and if it be for my good. You love me too much to let me suffer unless it be for my good. Therefore, O Lord, I trust myself to you; do with me as you please. In sickness and in health, I wish to love you always.

For Purity

O Jesus, most pure of heart! O spotless Lamb of God! Help me that I may keep my heart and body pure, that all through my life I may never displease you by any wicked thing. Give me the blessing of the clean of heart.

On going to bed

Into your hands, O Lord, I commend my spirit: Lord Jesus, receive my soul. In the name of our Lord Jesus Christ crucified, I lay me down to rest. Bless me, O Lord, and defend me; preserve me from a sudden and unprovided death and from all dangers, and bring me to life everlasting with you.

In Thanksgiving

My God, from my heart I thank you for the many blessings you have given to me. I thank you for having created and baptised me, and for having placed me in your holy Catholic Church; and for having given me so many graces and mercies through the merits of Jesus Christ. And I thank you, dear Jesus, for having become a little child for my sake, to teach me to be holy and humble like you; and for having died upon the Cross that I might have pardon for my sins and get to heaven. Also I thank you for all your other mercies, most of all for those you have given me today.

Prayer for the Pope

O almighty and eternal God, have mercy on your servant our Holy Father, the Pope, and direct him according to your clemency into the way of everlasting salvation; that he may desire by your grace those things that are agreeable to you, and perform them with all his strength. Through Christ our Lord. Amen.

Prayer for Priests

Father, you have appointed your Son Jesus Christ eternal High Priest. Guide those he has chosen to be ministers of word and sacrament and help them to be faithful in fulfilling the ministry they have received. Grant this through our Lord Jesus Christ, your Son, who lives and reigns with you and the Holy Spirit, one God, for ever and ever. Amen.

Prayer for Vocations

Lord Jesus Christ, Shepherd of souls, who called the apostles to be fishers of men, raise up new apostles in your holy Church. Teach them that to serve you is to reign: to possess you is to possess all things. Kindle in the young hearts of our sons and daughters the fire of zeal for souls. Make them eager to spread your Kingdom on earth. Grant them courage to follow you, who are the Way, the Truth and the Life; who live and reign for ever and ever. Amen. Mary, Queen of the Clergy, pray for us. Help our students who are preparing for the priesthood.

Prayer for Unity

O Lord Jesus Christ, who said to your apostles, peace I leave you, my peace I give to you; look not upon our sins, but upon the faith of your Church and grant to her that peace and unity which is according to your will; who live and reign for ever and ever. Amen.

Prayer for Peace

Give peace, O Lord, in our days; for there is no other to fight for us, but only you, our God.

V. May peace be ours through your protection,
O Lord.
R. And prosperity through your strong defence.

Let us pray:

O God, from whom are holy desires, right counsels and just deeds, give to your servants that peace which the world cannot give; that we may serve you with our whole hearts, and live quiet lives under your protection, free from the fear of our enemies. Through Christ our Lord. Amen.

Grace before and after meals

Bless us, O Lord, and these your gifts which we are about to receive from your bounty. Through Christ our Lord. Amen.

We give you thanks, almighty God, for all your benefits, who live and reign, for ever and ever.

✠ May the souls of the faithful departed, through the mercy of God, rest in peace. Amen.

The Litany of the Blessed Virgin

Lord have mercy.
Lord have mercy.
Christ have mercy.
Christ have mercy.
Lord have mercy.
Lord have mercy.
Christ hear us.
Christ graciously hear us.

God the Father of heaven,
have mercy on us.
God the Son, Redeemer of the world,
have mercy on us.
God the Holy Spirit,
have mercy on us.
Holy Trinity, one God,
have mercy on us.

Holy Mary,
pray for us.
Holy Mother of God,
pray for us.
Holy Virgin of virgins,
pray for us.
Mother of Christ,
pray for us.
Mother of divine grace,
pray for us.
Mother most pure,
pray for us.
Mother most chaste,
pray for us.
Mother inviolate,
pray for us.
Mother undefiled,
pray for us.
Mother most lovable,
pray for us.
Mother most admirable,
pray for us.
Mother of good counsel,
pray for us.
Mother of our Creator,
pray for us.
Mother of our Saviour,
pray for us.

Virgin most prudent,
pray for us.

The Litany of the Blessed Virgin

Virgin most venerable,
pray for us.
Virgin most renowned,
pray for us.
Virgin most powerful,
pray for us.
Virgin most merciful,
pray for us.
Virgin most faithful,
pray for us.

Mirror of Justice,
pray for us.
Seat of wisdom,
pray for us.
Cause of our joy,
pray for us.
Spiritual vessel,
pray for us.
Vessel of honour,
pray for us.
Singular vessel of devotion,
pray for us.
Mystical rose,
pray for us.
Tower of David,
pray for us.
Tower of ivory,
pray for us.
House of gold,
pray for us.
Ark of the covenant,
pray for us.
Gate of heaven,
pray for us.
Morning Star,
pray for us.
Health of the sick,
pray for us.
Refuge of sinners,
pray for us.
Comfort of the afflicted,
pray for us.
Help of Christians,
pray for us.

Queen of Angels,
pray for us.
Queen of Patriarchs,
pray for us.
Queen of Prophets,
pray for us.
Queen of Apostles

pray for us.
Queen of Martyrs, *pray for us.*
Queen of Confessors, *pray for us.*
Queen of Virgins, *pray for us.*
Queen of all Saints, *pray for us.*
Queen conceived without original sin, *pray for us*
Queen assumed into heaven, *pray for us.*
Queen of the most holy Rosary, *pray for us.*
Queen of Peace, *pray for us.*
Queen of the Family, *pray for us.*

Lamb of God, you take away the sins of the world, *spare us*, O Lord.
Lamb of God, you take away the sins of the world, *graciously hear us*, O Lord.
Lamb of God, you take away the sins of the world, *have mercy on us*.

V. Pray for us, O holy Mother of God.
R. That we may be made worthy of the promises of Christ.

Let us pray:
Lord God, give to your people the joy of continual health in mind and body. With the prayers of the Virgin Mary to help us, guide us through the sorrows of this life to eternal happiness in the life to come. Grant this through our Lord Jesus Christ, your Son, who lives and reigns with you and the Holy Spirit, one God, for ever and ever. **R.** Amen.

— ❧ Preparing for Confession ❧ —

Before Confession

Almighty and merciful God,
you have brought me here in the name of your Son
to receive your mercy and grace in my time of need.
Open my eyes to see the evil I have done.
Touch my heart and convert me to yourself.
Where sin separated me from you,
may your love unite me to you again:
where sin has brought weakness,
may your power heal and strengthen;
where sin has brought death,
may your Spirit raise to new life.
Give me a new heart to love you,
so that my life may reflect the image of your Son.
May the world see the glory
of Christ revealed in your Church,
and come to know that he is the one whom
you have sent, Jesus Christ, your Son, our Lord. Amen.

The following 'examination of conscience' is to help us to compare our lives with the example and commandments of Christ.
"You shall love the Lord your God with all your heart, and with all your soul, and with all your mind, and with all your strength."

- When making important decisions about my way of life, have I put God first?
- Am I so caught up with getting on in this world that I give no thought to the things of God?
- Have I risked losing my faith through pride or cowardice?
- Have I really trusted God, especially in times of difficulty?
- Have I prayed morning and evening and in times of temptation?
- Do I really love God's name? Have I been guilty of foul language, of contempt for God's name or sacred things? Swearing?
- Is Sunday (or a holy day) a day on which I try to give time and attention to the things of God and of my religion - particularly by taking a full and prayerful part in the Mass and receiving Communion with devotion?
- Is my heart set on money, on my own amusement at any cost?

Now consider the second great commandment:
"You shall love your neighbour as yourself."
- Do I use other people for my own ends and advantage?
- In my family life, do I really try to fulfil my responsibilities, as father or mother, husband or wife, son or daughter? Do I make my home a happy and loving place by being tolerant and forgiving? Have I tried to ensure a Christian upbringing for my children? Do I scandalize them in what I say or do in their presence?

Examination of Conscience

- Do I make it harder for them to grow up responsibly? Do I put temptation in their path - particularly by irresponsibly letting them go their own way?
- Have I been faithful to my husband or to my wife?
- Do I spend a proper amount of my wages or any other monies I have on the family, or do I spend it on other things? Do I gamble it away or spend it on luxuries for my own personal amusement to the harm of the home?
- Do I take a fair share of responsibility for older members of my family now grown old or infirm?
- Do I spend time and money on the less fortunate?
- Have I forgotten to help victims of oppression or poverty?
- Do I despise others, particularly those of other races or religions?
- Do I do my fair share working for the good of my parish contributing in some measure to the good of the whole Church? Do I selfishly stand aloof and neglect all appeals for help?
- Do I avoid getting involved with the people of my own area, at home or at work? Do I do nothing about obvious injustice suffered by others?
- Have I paid my taxes? Am I honest about them?
- In my work am I just, hard-working, honest? Do I cheat or break agreements or contracts?
- Do I break the laws enacted by legitimate authority?

- Do I drive dangerously? Have I driven when under the influence of drink? Do I refuse to pay my bills? Have I been truthful and fair? Have I deliberately deceived others? Judged them rashly? Injured their reputation by lies about them? Have I revealed secrets?
- Have I been guilty of physical violence? Caused physical damage? Maliciously ill-treated others?
- Do I hate people?
- Do I insult others, quarrel with them, lose my temper with them?
- Have I been responsible for advising/procuring an abortion?
- Have I stolen anything? Have I forgiven every injury?

And now let us remember what it means to be a true disciple of our Lord.
"If any man would come after me, let him deny himself and take up his cross and follow me."
- Do I deny myself? Do I eat or drink more than is reasonable? Am I envious, proud or arrogant?
- Am I lazy? Do I accept suffering and disappointment as a share in the Passion of Christ?
- Have I fasted and abstained when this has been asked of me by the Church?
- Have I been chaste and pure? Or have I toyed with temptations to impurity - by deliberately looking for what is impure?

- Have I dishonoured my body by fornication, impurity, foul conversation, lustful thoughts, unchaste actions?
- Have I given in to sensuality, particularly in my reading or my entertainments?
- Is my married life according to God's will and law?
- Have I used methods of birth control contrary to the Church's teaching on the place of sex in marriage?

THE SACRAMENT OF PENANCE

Pray now to God for the forgiveness of your sins, and that he may grant you the grace of a true change of heart and of a genuine determination to live your life according to our Lord's word. You could read something from Scripture, such as chapter 1 of the first letter of St John, to be found very near the end of the New Testament. When you are sure that you are sorry, you are ready to approach the priest. He welcomes you warmly in brotherly love. You make the sign of the cross, saying:

In the name of the Father, and of the Son, and of the Holy Spirit. Amen.

The priest will then briefly invite you to have confidence and trust in God.

You reply: **Amen.**

Next tell the priest about yourself, unless he already knows you. You should tell him anything which may help him to help you in your spiritual life; for instance, when you last went to confession, whether you are married or not, and the main difficulties which you have in trying to live the Christian life.

Then the priest, or you yourself at his invitation, may choose to celebrate a Liturgy of the Word by reading an appropriate passage of Holy Scripture proclaiming God's mercy and calling men to conversion. The passages which appear in 'A Simple Penance Book' (from CTS) are the same as those in the book which the priest is using.

The Sacrament of Penance

You may if you wish now say a general formula for confession (for an example see page 6, the Confiteor). Then confess your sins, and listen to any advice the priest may give you. After this accept the penance the priest will propose and express your sorrow in any words you choose (See pages 6 and 11 for Acts of Contrition). Listen carefully to the words of Absolution and at the end reply: **Amen.**

The rite of Penance concludes with a proclamation of praise of God. The priest may say:

Give thanks to the Lord, for he is good.

You reply: **His mercy endures for ever.**

Then the priest dismisses you saying:

The Lord has freed you from your sins. Go in peace.

In place of the proclamation of God's praise and the dismissal, the priest may use any one of four other given texts. None of them requires any reply from you.

After Confession

After leaving the place of confession you have the opportunity to reflect on what has taken place and to thank God for his mercy and forgiveness in the quiet of the church You are once again part of the mystery of salvation. Here is a prayer of thanksgiving:

Father, in your love you have brought me from evil to good and from misery to happiness. Through your blessings give me the courage of perseverance. Amen.

Prayers for
❧ Holy Communion ❧

Say these Prayers slowly, a few words at a time. It is well to stop after every few words, that they may sink into the heart. Each Prayer may be said several times.

Before Holy Communion

Prayer for Help. O God, help me to make a good Communion. Mary, my dearest mother, pray to Jesus for me. My dear Angel Guardian, lead me to the Altar of God.

Act of Faith. O God, because you have said it, I believe that I shall receive the Sacred Body of Jesus Christ to eat, and his Precious Blood to drink. My God, I believe this with all my heart.

Act of Humility. My God, I confess that I am a poor sinner; I am not worthy to receive the Body and Blood of Jesus, on account of my sins. Lord, I am not worthy to receive you under my roof; but only say the word, and my soul will be healed.

Act of Sorrow. My God, I detest all the sins of my life. I am sorry for them, because they have offended you, my God, you who are so good. I resolve never to commit sin any more. My good God, pity me, have mercy on me, forgive me.

Act of Adoration. O Jesus, great God, present on the Altar, I bow down before you. I adore you.

Act of Love and Desire. Jesus, I love you. I desire with all my heart to receive you. Jesus, come into my poor soul, and give me your Flesh to eat and your Blood to drink. Give me your whole Self, Body, Blood, Soul and Divinity, that I may live for ever with you.

Receiving Holy Communion

Answer Amen *when the priest says* The Body of Christ. *You are free to receive the Sacred Host either directly on to your tongue or in your open hand, as you prefer. In the latter case, pick it up straight away with your other hand, and place it reverently on your tongue yourself. Jesus is now really present in you. Keep away all earthly thoughts and enjoy his presence. If you are to receive Holy Communion under both kinds separately, answer* Amen *when the priest or deacon says* The Blood of Christ. *You will be handed the chalice; you should lift the chalice with your own hands and drink a little of the Precious Blood, being careful not to spill any. If you receive Holy Communion under both kinds together (called 'by intinction') the priest will say* The Body and Blood of Christ *(answer* Amen*) and he will then give you the Sacred Host on to your tongue after he has dipped it in the consecrated wine.*

After Holy Communion

Act of Faith. O Jesus, I believe that I have received your Flesh to eat and your Blood to drink, because you have said it, and your word is true. All that I have and all that I am are your gift and now you have given me yourself.

Act of Adoration. O Jesus, my God, my Creator, I adore you, because from your hands I came and with you I am to be happy for ever.

Act of Humility. O Jesus, I am not worthy to receive you, and yet you have come to me that my poor heart may learn of you to be meek and humble.

Act of Love. Jesus, I love you; I love you with all my heart. You know that I love you, and wish to love you daily more and more.

Act of Thanksgiving. My good Jesus, I thank you with all my heart. How good, how kind you are to me. Blessed be Jesus in the most holy Sacrament of the Altar.

Act of Offering. O Jesus, receive my poor offering. Jesus, you have given yourself to me, and now let me give myself to you:
    I give you my body, that I may be chaste and pure.
    I give you my soul, that I may be free from sin.
    I give you my heart, that I may always love you.

I give you my every breath that I shall breathe,
and especially my last.
I give you myself in life and in death,
that I may be yours for ever and ever.

Pray for Others

O Jesus, have mercy on your holy Church; take care of it.
O Jesus, have pity on poor sinners, and save them from hell.
O Jesus, bless my father, my mother, my brothers and sisters, and all I ought to pray for, as your Heart knows how to bless them.
O Jesus, have pity on the poor souls in purgatory and give them eternal rest.

Pray for Yourself

O Jesus, wash away my sins with your Precious Blood.
O Jesus, the struggle against temptation is not yet finished. My Jesus, when temptation comes near me, make me strong against it. In the moment of temptation may I always say: "My Jesus, mercy! Mary, help!"
O Jesus, may I lead a good life; may I die a happy death. May I receive you before I die. May I say when I am dying: "Jesus, Mary and Joseph, I give you my heart and my soul".

Listen now for a moment to Jesus Christ; perhaps he has something to say to you. Answer Jesus in your heart, and tell him all your troubles. Then say:

Jesus, I am going away for a time, but I trust not without you. You are with me by your grace. I resolve never to leave you by mortal sin. Although I am so weak I have such hope in you. Give me grace to persevere. Amen.

Anima Christi

Soul of Christ, be my sanctification.
Body of Christ, be my salvation.
Blood of Christ, fill all my veins.
Water from the side of Christ, wash out my stains.
May Christ's Passion strengthen me,
O good Jesu, hear me.
In thy wounds I fain would hide,
Never to be parted from thy side.
Guard me when my foes assail me.
Call me when my life shall fail me.
Command me then to come to thee.
That I for all eternity
With thy saints may praise thee.
Amen. *(Cardinal Newman)*

Prayer before a Crucifix

Behold, O kind and most sweet Jesus, I cast myself on my knees in your sight, and with the most fervent desire of my soul, I pray and beseech you that you would impress upon my heart lively sentiments of faith, hope, and charity, with a true repentance for my sins, and a firm desire of amendment, while with deep affection and grief of soul I ponder within myself and mentally contemplate your five most precious wounds; having before my eyes that which David spoke in prophecy of you, O good Jesus: 'They pierced my hands and my feet; they have numbered all my bones'.

(A plenary indulgence, under the usual conditions (see page 52), is attached to the recitation of this prayer on the Fridays in Lent and Passiontide. At other times a partial indulgence can be obtained.)

❧ BENEDICTION ❧

As the Blessed Sacrament is being brought to, or placed on, the altar, the following or another Eucharistic hymn is sung:

O salutáris hóstia,	O saving Victim, opening wide
Quæ cæli pandis óstium;	The gate of heaven to man below;
Bella premunt hostília,	Our foes press on from every side;
Da robur, fer auxílium.	Thine aid supply, thy strength bestow.
Uni Trinóque Dómino	To thy great name be endless praise,
Sit sempitérna glória,	Immortal Godhead, one in three;
Qui vitam sine término	O grant us endless length of days
Nobis donet in pátria.	In our true native land with thee.
Amen.	Amen.

During exposition there may be readings, prayers (for example the Divine Praises, page 36) and periods of silent adoration. Towards the end of exposition the priest or deacon goes to the altar and kneels. Another Eucharistic hymn is sung, for example the following:

BENEDICTION

Tantum ergo Sacraméntum	Therefore we, before him bending,
Venerémur cérnui:	This great Sacrament revere;
Et antíquum documéntum	Types and shadows have their ending,
Novo cedit rítui:	For the newer rite is here;
Præstet fides suppleméntum	Faith, our outward sense befriending,
Sénsuum deféctui.	Makes the inward vision clear.
Genitóri, Genitóque	Glory let us give, and blessing
Laus et jubilátio.	To the Father and the Son;
Salus, honor, virtus quoque	Honour, might, and praise addressing,
Sit et benedíctio;	While eternal ages run;
Procedénti ab utróque,	Ever too his love confessing,
Compar sit laudátio.	Who, from both, with both is one.
Amen.	Amen.

The following or another Prayer is said: Lord Jesus Christ, you gave us the Eucharist as the memorial of your suffering and death. May our worship of this sacrament of your body and blood help us to experience the salvation you won for us and the peace of the kingdom where you live with the Father and the Holy Spirit, one God, for ever and ever. Amen.

The priest blesses the people with the Blessed Sacrament, while an acclamation is sung or said.

Ant. Adorémus in ætérnum sanctíssimum Sacraméntum.	*Ant.* Let us adore for ever the most holy Sacrament.
Ps. Laudáte Dóminum, omnes gentes; laudáte eum omnes pópuli.	*Ps.* O praise the Lord, all you nations; praise him, all you people.
Quóniam confirmáta est super nos misericórdia ejus; et véritas Dómini manet in ætérnum.	For his mercy is confirmed upon us; and the truth of the Lord remains for ever.
Glória Patri, et Filio, et Spirítui Sancto.	Glory be to the Father, and to the Son, and to the Holy Spirit.
Sicut erat in princípio, et nunc, et semper, et in sǽcula sæculórum. Amen.	As it was in the beginning, is now, and ever shall be, world without end. Amen.
Ant. Adorémus in ætérnum sanctíssimum Sacraméntum.	*Ant.* Let us adore for ever the most holy Sacrament.

The Divine Praises

Blessed be God.
Blessed be his holy Name.
Blessed be Jesus Christ, true God and true Man.
Blessed be the name of Jesus.

Blessed be his most Sacred Heart.
Blessed be his most Precious Blood.
Blessed be Jesus in the most holy Sacrament of the Altar.
Blessed be the Holy Spirit, the Paraclete.
Blessed be the great Mother of God, Mary most holy.
Blessed be her holy and Immaculate Conception.
Blessed be her glorious Assumption.
Blessed be the name of Mary, Virgin and Mother.
Blessed be St Joseph, her spouse most chaste.
Blessed be God in his Angels and in his Saints.

Prayer for England

O Blessed Virgin Mary, Mother of God and our most gentle Queen and Mother, look down in mercy upon England, your Dowry, and upon us all who greatly hope and trust in you. By you it was that Jesus, our Saviour and hope, was given to the world; and he has given you to us that we may hope still more. Plead for us your children, whom you did receive and accept at the foot of the Cross, O sorrowful Mother. Intercede for our separated brethren, that with us in the one true fold they may be united to the Chief Shepherd, the Vicar of your Son. Pray for us all, dear Mother, that by faith fruitful in good works we may all deserve to see and praise God, together with you in our heavenly home. Amen.

The Way of the Cross

I. Jesus is condemned to death.
Consider how Jesus, after having been scourged and crowned with thorns, was unjustly condemned by Pilate to die on the Cross.

II. Jesus Receives the Cross.
Consider how Jesus, in making this journey with the Cross on his shoulders, thought of us, and offered for us to his Father the death he was about to undergo.

III. Jesus falls the first time under his Cross.
Consider the first fall of Jesus under his Cross. His flesh was torn by the scourges, his head was crowned with thorns; he had lost a great quantity of blood. So weakened he could scarcely walk, he yet had to carry this great load upon his shoulders. The soldiers struck him rudely, and he fell several times.

IV. Jesus is met by his Blessed Mother.
Consider this meeting of the Son and the Mother, which took place on this journey. Their looks became like so many arrows to wound those hearts which loved each other so tenderly.

V. The Cross is laid upon Simon of Cyrene.
Consider how his cruel tormentors, seeing that Jesus was on the point of expiring, and fearing he would die on the way, whereas they wished him to die the shameful death of the Cross, constrained Simon of Cyrene to carry the Cross behind our Lord.

VI. Veronica wipes the face of Jesus.
Consider how the holy woman named Veronica, seeing Jesus so ill-used, and bathed in sweat and blood, wiped his face with a towel, on which was left the impression of his holy countenance.

VII. Jesus falls the second time.
Consider the second fall of Jesus under the Cross; a fall which renews the pain of all the wounds in his head and members.

VIII. The women of Jerusalem mourn for our Lord.
Consider how these women wept with compassion at seeing Jesus in such a pitiable state, streaming with blood, as he walked along. 'Daughters of Jerusalem', said he, 'weep not for me, but for yourselves and for your children'.

IX. Jesus falls for the third time.
Consider the third fall of Jesus Christ. His weakness was extreme, and the cruelty of his executioners excessive, who tried to hasten his steps when he could scarcely move.

X. Jesus is stripped of his garments.
Consider the violence with which Jesus was stripped by the executioners. His inner garments adhered to his torn flesh, and they dragged them off so roughly that the skin came with them. Take pity on your Saviour thus cruelly treated.

XI. Jesus is nailed to the Cross.
Consider how Jesus, having been placed upon the Cross, extended his hands, and offered to his Eternal Father the sacrifice of his life for our salvation. Those barbarians fastened him with nails, and then, securing the Cross, allowed him to die with anguish on this infamous gibbet.

XII. Jesus dies on the Cross.
Consider how Jesus, being consumed with the anguish after three hours' agony on the Cross, abandoned himself to the weight of his body, bowed his head and died.

XIII. Jesus is taken down from the Cross.
Consider how, after our Lord had expired, two of his disciples, Joseph and Nicodemus, took him down from the Cross and placed him in the arms of his afflicted Mother, who received him with unutterable tenderness, and pressed him to her bosom.

XIV. Jesus is placed in the sepulchre.
Consider how the disciples, accompanied by his holy Mother, carried the body of Jesus to bury it. They closed the tomb, and all came sorrowfully away.

The Holy Rosary

The Holy Rosary is composed of fifteen decades, each decade consisting of the Our Father, ten Hail Marys, and the Glory be to the Father, and each being recited in honour of some mystery in the life of our Lord and of his Blessed Mother. During each decade we should call to mind the mystery which it is intended to honour, and pray that we may learn to practise the virtue specially taught us by that mystery.

I. The Five Joyful Mysteries

1. The Annunciation.
2. The Visitation.
3. The Nativity.
4. The Presentation in the Temple.
5. The Finding of the Child Jesus in the Temple.

II. The Five Sorrowful Mysteries

1. The Prayer and Agony in the Garden.
2. The Scourging at the Pillar.
3. The Crowning with Thorns.
4. The Carrying of the Cross.
5. The Crucifixion and Death of our Lord.

III. The Five Glorious Mysteries

1. The Resurrection.
2. The Ascension of Christ into Heaven.
3. The Descent of the Holy Spirit on the Apostles.
4. The Assumption.
5. The Coronation of the Blessed Virgin Mary in Heaven and the Glory of all the Saints.

Then is said:
Hail, holy Queen, mother of mercy; hail our life, our sweetness, and our hope! To you do we cry, poor banished children of Eve; to you do we send up our sighs, mourning and weeping in this vale of tears. Turn then, most gracious advocate, your eyes of mercy towards us; and after this our exile, show us the blessed fruit of your womb, Jesus.
O clement, O loving, O sweet Virgin Mary.

V. Pray for us, O holy Mother of God.
R. That we may be made worthy of the promises of Christ.
Let us pray.
O God, whose only-begotten Son, by his life, death and resurrection, has purchased for us the rewards of eternal life; grant, we beseech you, that meditating on these Mysteries of the most holy Rosary of the Blessed Virgin

Mary, we may both imitate what they contain, and obtain what they promise, through the same Christ our Lord.
R. Amen.

(A plenary indulgence may be gained, under the usual conditions (see page 52), for the recitation of the Rosary (five decades are sufficient), in a church or public oratory or in the family. If the Rosary is said privately a partial indulgence may be gained.)

A Quarter of an Hour Before
⁂ The Blessed Sacrament ⁂

To please Me, dear child, it is not necessary to know much; all that is required is to love Me much, to be deeply sorry for ever having offended Me and desirous of being ever faithful to Me in future.

Speak to Me now as you would do to your dearest friend. Tell Me all that now fills your mind and heart. Are there any you wish to commend to Me? Tell Me their names, and tell Me what you would wish Me to do for them. Do not fear, ask for much; I love generous hearts, which, forgetting themselves, wish well to others.

Speak to Me of the poor you wish to comfort; tell Me of the sick that you would wish to see relieved. Ask of Me something for those who have been unkind to you, or who have crossed you. Ask much for them all; commend them with all your heart to Me.

And ask Me many graces for yourself. Are there not many graces you would wish to name that would make you happier in yourself, more useful and pleasing to others, more worthy of the love of Me, the dearest Lord, Master, and Spouse of your soul? Tell Me the whole list of the favours you want of Me. Tell Me them with humility, knowing how poor you are without them, how unable to gain them by yourself; ask for them with much love, that they may make you more pleasing to Me. With all a child's simplicity, tell Me how self-seeking you are, how proud, vain, irritable, how cowardly in sacrifice, how lazy in work, uncertain in your good resolutions, and then ask Me to bless and crown your efforts. Poor child, fear not, blush not at the sight of so many failings; there are Saints in heaven who had the faults you have; they came to Me lovingly, they prayed earnestly to Me, and My grace has made them good and holy in My sight.

You should be Mine, body and soul; fear not, therefore, to ask of Me gifts of body and mind, health, judgment, memory, and success - ask for them for My sake; that God may be glorified in all things. I can grant everything, and never refuse to give what may make a soul dearer to Me and better able to fulfil the will of God.

Have you no plans for the future which occupy, perhaps distress, your mind? Tell Me your hopes, your fears. Is it about your future state? Your position among My creatures? Some good you wish to bring to others? In what shall I help and bless your good will?

And for Me you must have - have you not? - some zeal, some wish to do good to the souls of others. Some, perhaps, who love and care for you, have ceased, almost, to know or care for Me. Shall I give you strength, wisdom and tact, to bring these poor ones close to My heart again? Have you failed in the past? Tell me how you acted; I will show you why you did not gain all you expected; rely on Me, I will help you, and will guide you to lead others to Me.

And what crosses have you, My dear child? Have they been many and heavy ones? Has someone caused you pain? Someone wounded your self-love? slighted you? injured you? Lay your head upon My breast, and tell Me how you suffered. Have you felt that some have been ungrateful to you, and unfeeling towards you? Tell Me all, and in the warmth of My heart you will find strength to forgive and even to forget that they have ever wished to pain you.

And what fears have you, My child? My providence shall comfort you. My love sustain you. I am never away from you, never can abandon you. Are some growing cold in the interest and love they had for you? Pray to Me for them; I will restore them to you if it be better for you and your sanctification.

Have you got some happiness to make known to Me? What happened since you came to Me last, to console you, to gladden and give you joy? What was it? a mark of true friendship you received? a success unexpected and almost unhoped for? a fear suddenly taken away from you? and did you remember the while, that in all it was My will, My love, that brought all that your heart has been so glad to have? It was My hand, My dear child, that guided and prepared all for you. Look to Me now, My child, and say: 'Dear Jesus, I thank you'.

A Visit to the Blessed Sacrament

You will soon leave Me now; what promises can you make me? Let them be sincere ones, humble ones, full of love and desire to please Me. Tell Me how carefully you will avoid every occasion of sin, drive from you all that leads to harm, and shun the world - the great deceiver of souls. Promise to be kind to the poor; loving, for My sake, to friends; forgiving to your enemies, and charitable to all, not in word alone and actions, but in your very thoughts. When you have little love for your neighbour, whom you see, you are forgetting Me who am hidden from you.

Love all My Saints; seek the help of your holy patrons. I love to glorify them by giving you much through them. Love, above all, My own sweet glorious Mother - she is your mother; love her, speak to her often, and she will bring you to Me, and for her sake, I will love and bless you more each day.

Return soon to Me again, but come with your heart empty of the world, for I have many more favours to give, more than you can know of; bring your heart so that I may fill it with many gifts of My love.

My peace be with you.

Summary of
❧ Christian Doctrine ❧

1. We are bound to know and to believe that: (1) There is one supreme, eternal, infinite God, the Creator of heaven and earth; and that the good will be rewarded by him for ever in heaven, and the wicked, who die unrepentant, will be punished for ever in hell. We believe in heaven and hell equally on the simple word of Christ. (2) In the Holy Trinity there are three Persons, co-eternal, co-equal: God the Father, God the Son, and God the Holy Spirit. (3) God the Son, the Second Person of the Holy Trinity, was made Man, and died upon the Cross to save us.

2. We are bound to know and believe the Apostles' Creed (page 5); and to have a knowledge of the Commandments of God and of the Church, and of the Holy Sacraments; especially of the necessity of Baptism and that the Eucharist is a pledge of our future glory. We must believe that Sacred Tradition and Sacred Scripture form one sacred deposit of the word of God, which is committed to the Church. We should know the Lord's Prayer and the Hail Mary.

3. We are bound, moreover, to believe whatever God teaches us by his holy Church, who in her teaching cannot deceive us nor be deceived. Her teaching is, among other ways, infallibly made known to us by the Pope when he speaks *ex cathedra* - that is, when discharging the office of Pastor and teacher of all Christians, he defines, by virtue of his supreme apostolic authority, a doctrine regarding faith or morals, to be held by the universal Church. Infallibility resides also in the body of Bishops when that body exercises supreme teaching authority with the Pope, the successor of St Peter, as, for example, when gathered together in a General Council.

The Seven Sacraments

1. *Baptism*: by which we are made Christians, children of God, members of his holy Church, and heirs of heaven.

2. *Confirmation*: by which we receive the Holy Spirit, to make us strong and perfect Christians, and soldiers of Christ.

3. *The Holy Eucharist*: which is really and truly and substantially the Body and Blood, the Soul and Divinity, of Jesus Christ, under the appearances of bread and wine. The Holy Eucharist is not only a Sacrament, in which we receive our divine Lord for the food and nourishment of our souls, and in which he is really present to be adored upon the altar; it is also a Sacrifice, the Sacrifice of the Holy Mass, in which, at the time of consecration, the bread and wine are changed into the Body and Blood of Jesus Christ, and in which he is offered up for us to his eternal Father.

4. *Penance*: by which the sins committed after Baptism are forgiven.

5. *Anointing of the Sick*: which, in dangerous illness, and in preparation for death, comforts the soul, remits sins, and restores health if God sees this to be expedient.

6. *Holy Orders*: by which Bishops, Priests, and Deacons receive power and grace to perform their sacred duties.

7. *Matrimony*: which is the Sacrament of Christian Marriage.

The Ten Commandments of God

1. I am the Lord your God: you shall not have strange gods before me.

2. You shall not take the name of the Lord your God in vain.

3. Remember to keep holy the Lord's day.

4. Honour your father and your mother.

5. You shall not kill.

6. You shall not commit adultery.

7. You shall not steal.

8. You shall not bear false witness against your neighbour.

9. You shall not covet your neighbour's wife.

10. You shall not covet your neighbour's goods.

A Summary of Christian Doctrine

The Six Chief Commandments of the Church

1. To keep the Sundays and holy days of Obligation holy, by hearing Mass and resting from servile works.

2. To keep the days of Fasting and Abstinence appointed by the Church.

3. To go to Confession when we are conscious of having sinned gravely.

4. To receive the Blessed Sacrament at least once a year, at Easter or thereabouts.

5. To contribute to the support of our pastors.

6. Not to marry within certain degrees of kindred without dispensation.

The Three Theological Virtues: Faith, Hope, and Charity.

The Four Cardinal Virtues: Prudence, Justice, Fortitude, and Temperance.

The Seven Gifts of the Holy Spirit: Wisdom, Understanding, Counsel, Fortitude, Knowledge, Piety, the Fear of the Lord.

The Twelve Fruits of the Holy Spirit: Charity, Joy, Peace, Patience, Benignity, Goodness, Longanimity, Mildness, Faith, Modesty, Continency, Chastity.

The Seven Corporal Works of Mercy: To feed the hungry; to give drink to the thirsty; to clothe the naked; to harbour the harbourless; the visit the sick; to visit the imprisoned; to bury the dead.

The Seven Spiritual Works of Mercy: To counsel the doubtful; to instruct the ignorant; to admonish sinners; to comfort the afflicted; to forgive offences; to bear wrongs patiently; to pray for the living and the dead.

The Seven Deadly Sins: Pride, Avarice, Lust, Anger, Gluttony, Envy, Sloth.

The Opposite Virtues: Humility, Liberality, Chastity, Meekness, Temperance, Brotherly Love, Diligence.

Indulgences

An indulgence is a remission granted by the Church to those who are free from the guilt of mortal sin, of the whole, or of a part, of the temporal punishment due for sins already forgiven.

(1) By temporal punishment, as distinguished from eternal punishment, is meant punishment which is due for sin, and which will come to an end, either in this world, or in the next world in purgatory. The repentance for sin may be so great as to obtain from God the remission both of the guilt and of all punishment; but often through imperfection of our repentance some punishment remains due for sin after the guilt has been removed.

(2) Indulgences are granted on the condition of the performance of certain specified good works; and they cannot be gained by anyone who is not free from the guilt of all grievous sins. (3) The Church, in granting an indulgence, offers to God, for the remission of the temporal punishment deserved for our sins, the infinite superabundant merits of our Lord, and also, in him and through him (though only secondarily), the merits of the Blessed Virgin and the Saints. (4) A plenary indulgence is a remission of the whole of the punishment due for forgiven sins; a partial indulgence is a remission of some part of that punishment. An indulgence granted as plenary will, if there be an obstacle to its full effect, be only partially obtained. A partial indulgence adds to any indulgenced act the same remission of temporal punishment as had been obtained by the performance of the action itself

The usual conditions for gaining a plenary indulgence are, in addition to the good work to which it is attached: (1) *Confession* on the day itself, or within some days before or after the performance of the good work. (2) *Holy Communion* on the day itself, or within some days before or after the performance of the good work. (3) *Prayer for the intention of the Pope*. For this, recitation of one Our Father and one Hail Mary suffices, though the faithful have the liberty of saying any other prayer according to their personal piety.

It is recommended that the Holy Communion and the prayer for the Pope's intention take place on the same day as the good work. Only one plenary indulgence may be gained on any one day with the exception of the plenary indulgence applicable at the moment of death. One sacramental Confession suffices to gain several plenary indulgences. But for each plenary indulgence Communion must be received and prayer for the Pope's intention must be said.

All indulgences may be applied to the faithful departed.

❧ Marriage & the Church ❧

1. Marriage between Catholics, or between a Catholic and a non-Catholic, should generally be celebrated before a duly authorised Priest or Deacon, and two witnesses. A marriage between two non-Catholics is not subject to this rule.

2. In this context a Catholic means anyone baptised in the Catholic Church.

3. A 'mixed marriage' is a marriage between a Catholic and a non-Catholic. The Church is prepared to grant a dispensation for such marriages on the following conditions:

(a) The Catholic must make a sincere promise, normally in writing, to preserve his/her Catholic faith and to do all in his/her power to have any children who may be born of the marriage baptised and brought up in the Catholic Church, and the non-Catholic must be made aware of his/her undertaking. If the non-Catholic is conscientiously opposed to the Catholic's obligations in this matter, the full situation must be referred to the Bishop.

(b) The marriage ceremony must take place in the Catholic Church. For cogent reasons, however, and with a special dispensation, a Catholic can contract a valid marriage with a non-Catholic in a non-Catholic church.

Note: It is advisable for persons intending to marry to give at least three months notice to the Parish Priest before the date of the marriage.

❧ Fasting and Abstinence ❧

The age at which abstinence becomes binding is fourteen. The obligation of fasting is restricted to those who have completed their eighteenth year and it continues until they have begun their sixtieth.

Fasting and Abstinence are binding throughout the Church on Ash Wednesday and Good Friday only.

In England and Wales and in Scotland, whilst abstinence is not of obligation on the other Fridays, these are days on which self-denial should be practised. The form of self-denial, to be offered in union with our Lord's suffering and death on the Cross, is left to the free choice of each individual.

The Eucharistic Fast

(1) Water (and medicine) may be taken at any time.

(2) Solid food and drinks may be taken up to one hour before Holy Communion.

(3) Those who are advanced in age or who suffer from any infirmity, as well as those who take care of them, can receive Holy Communion even if they have taken something during the previous hour.

❧ Holy Mass ❧

The first commandment of the Church binds all Catholics to attend Mass on all Sundays and Holy days of Obligation.

This is a grave obligation on our conscience, unless some really serious cause prevents us. To come in late, wilfully or through carelessness, when Mass has begun, is at least a venial sin. To miss Mass when you cannot help it, or when it would be very difficult for you to attend Mass, is not a sin. So, if you were to miss Mass because you were ill, or because you had to stay at home to mind a sick person or children, or because you were a very long way from church, or if for some other reason you could not go, it would not be a sin. When you cannot go to Mass, say the Mass prayers yourself at home, if possible.

In *England and Wales,* the Holy days of Obligation are: The Epiphany (6 January); Ascension Day (forty days after Easter Sunday); Corpus Christi (the Thursday after Trinity Sunday); SS. Peter and Paul (29 June), the Assumption (15 August); All Saints (1 November); Christmas Day (25 December).

In Scotland, the Epiphany is kept on the Sunday after 1 January and Corpus Christi on the Sunday after Trinity Sunday. When a day of obligation (except Christmas) falls on Saturday or Monday, it is not of obligation in that year.

In Ireland, the Immaculate Conception of the Blessed Virgin Mary (8 December) and the Feast of St Patrick (17

March) are also Holy days of obligation, but the Feast of SS. Peter and Paul is not. All are observed on the actual day: there is no transference or omission.

The Mass Simply Explained

At the Last Supper, Jesus gave us the elements of a sacred rite which we were to do in memory of him and which would make his sacrificial death on the cross present to all people in every age.

First he preached the word of God to his disciples, giving them the new commandment of love. He prayed for them and for all those who through them would believe in Him. He prayed for the unity of all believers.

In the liturgy of the Mass this is represented by the Service of the Word of God. We listen to God's word in the scriptures and the homily, we express our faith in his word, and in the Prayer of the Faithful pray for the needs of all God's people.

Then he took bread and a cup of wine. This action of Christ is represented in the liturgy of the Mass by the rite of the Offertory, or the presentation of the gifts. Bread and wine are brought to the altar and the priest takes them and blesses God for them, for they are to become the body of Christ that was offered for us on the cross and his blood that was shed for us and for all men so that sins might be forgiven. In Communion they are to become for us "the bread of life" and "our spiritual drink".

He said the prayer of blessing over them. In the Mass this is the Eucharistic Prayer, which praises and thanks God for all his gifts and most especially for what Jesus achieved by his life, death and resurrection. The Holy Spirit is called down upon the gifts so that they may become Christ's body and blood and we may receive them worthily and fruitfully. Then, after the Consecration, they are offered to God the Father for the whole world and for the needs of the living and the dead.

He broke the bread and gave it to his disciples; he gave them the cup to drink. This is the rite of Communion which gives us the fruits of Christ's sacrifice in a holy meal. In receiving the body and blood of Christ we are united with Christ and with one another in Christ, and we are given a foretaste of the joy that will be ours when we are united for ever with Christ in the glory of his heavenly kingdom

Prayer before Mass

O God, to whom every heart is open, every desire known and from whom no secrets are hidden; purify the thoughts of our hearts by the inspiration of your Holy Spirit, that we may perfectly love you, and worthily praise your holy name. Amen.

— ⁂ The Order of the Mass ⁂ —
(with a Congregation)

The Introductory Rite

The Mass may begin with the singing or reciting of the Entrance Antiphon or a Hymn whilst the priest and servers approach the altar. The people stand. The priest kisses the altar, goes to his chair and stands facing the people.

Priest: In the name of the Father, and of the Son,
✠ and of the Holy Spirit.
Response: **Amen.**

The priest then welcomes all present with one of the following Greetings:

1. Pr. The grace of our Lord Jesus Christ and the love of God and the fellowship of the Holy Spirit be with you all.
R. And also with you.

2. Pr. The grace and peace of God our Father and the Lord Jesus Christ be with you.
R. Blessed be God, the Father of our Lord Jesus Christ. *Or:* **And also with you.**

3. Pr. The Lord be with you.
R. And also with you.

THE ORDER OF THE MASS

After the Greeting the Entrance Antiphon may be read by the priest if it has not already been said or sung. The priest may now comment briefly on the Mass of the day.

The Act of Penance

Then follows the Act of Penance. One of the following forms is used:

The priest invites the people to repent of their sins:
1. Pr. My brothers and sisters *(or similar wording)*, to prepare ourselves to celebrate the sacred mysteries, let us call to mind our sins.

After a brief silence all say:
I confess to almighty God, and to you, my brothers and sisters, that I have sinned through my own fault in my thoughts and in my words, in what I have done, and in what I have failed to do; and I ask blessed Mary, ever Virgin, all the angels and saints, and you, my brothers and sisters, to pray for me to the Lord our God.

The priest now gives the Absolution:
    Pr. May almighty God have mercy on us, forgive us our sins, and bring us to everlasting life.
    R. Amen.

2. Pr. My brothers and sisters *(or similar wording)*, to prepare ourselves to celebrate the sacred mysteries, let us call to mind our sins.

After a brief silence, the priest continues:
 Pr. Lord, we have sinned against you: Lord, have mercy.
 R. Lord, have mercy.
 Pr. Lord, show us your mercy and love.
 R. And grant us your salvation.

The priest now gives the Absolution:
 Pr. May almighty God have mercy on us, forgive us our sins, and bring us to everlasting life.
 R. Amen.

---

3. Pr. My brothers and sisters *(or similar wording)*, to prepare ourselves to celebrate the sacred mysteries, let us call to mind our sins.
After a brief silence the priest makes the following (or other) invocations followed by Lord, have mercy.
 Pr. You were sent to heal the contrite: Lord, have mercy.
 R. Lord, have mercy.
 Pr. You came to call sinners: Christ, have mercy.
 R. Christ, have mercy.
 Pr. You plead for us at the right hand of the Father: Lord, have mercy.
 R. Lord, have mercy.

The Order of the Mass

The priest now gives the Absolution:
Pr. May almighty God have mercy on us, forgive us our sins, and bring us to everlasting life.
R. Amen.

The Kýrie eléison now follows unless it has already been used in one of the forms of the Act of Penance.

Pr. Kýrie, eléison.	**Lord, have mercy.**
R. Kýrie, eléison.	**Lord, have mercy.**
Pr. Christe, eléison.	**Christ, have mercy.**
R. Christe, eléison.	**Christ, have mercy.**
Pr. Kýrie, eléison.	**Lord, have mercy.**
R. Kýrie, eléison.	**Lord, have mercy.**

The Gloria

Then follows the Gloria, when it is prescribed

Glória in excélsis Deo et in terra pax homínibus bonæ voluntátis. Laudámus te, benedícimus te, adorámus te, glorificámus te, grátias ágimus tibi propter magnam glóriam tuam, Dómine Deus, Rex cæléstis, Deus Pater omnípotens. Dómine Fili unigénite, Jesu Christe,

Glory to God in the highest, and peace to his people on earth. Lord God, heavenly King, almighty God and Father, we worship you, we give you thanks, we praise you for your glory, Lord Jesus Christ, only Son of the Father, Lord God, Lamb of God, you take away

Dómine Deus, Agnus Dei, Fílius Patris, qui tollis peccáta mundi, miserére nobis; qui tollis peccáta mundi, súscipe deprecatiónem nostram. Qui sedes ad déxteram Patris, miserére nobis. Quóniam tu solus Sanctus, tu solus Dóminus, tu solus Altissimus, Jesu Christe, cum Sancto Spíritu: in glória Dei Patris. Amen.

the sin of the world: have mercy on us; you are seated and the right hand of the Father; receive our prayer. For you alone are the Holy One, you alone are the Lord, you alone are the Most High, Jesus Christ, with the Holy Spirit, in the glory of God the Father. Amen.

The priest then says: Let us pray.
All pray silently with the priest for a while. Then the priest says the Collect which ends:

Pr. For ever and ever.
R. Amen.

The Liturgy of the Word

The people now sit for the first Reading. At the end of which the reader says:

This is the word of the Lord.
R. Thanks be to God.

Then follows the Psalm and the people make the Response. If there is a second Reading, it ends as before:

This is the word of the Lord.
R. Thanks be to God.

The Alleluia or another Chant may now follow. The people stand. The priest then bows before the altar and say silently:

Almighty God, cleanse my heart and my lips that I may worthily proclaim your Gospel.

Pr. The Lord be with you.
R. And also with you.
Pr. A reading from the Holy Gospel according to *N*.
R. Glory be to you, Lord.

At the end of the Gospel:

Pr. This is the Gospel of the Lord.
R. Praise to you, Lord Jesus Christ.

The priest kisses the book and says silently:

Pr. May the words of the Gospel wipe away our sins.

A Sermon follows on all Sundays and Holy days of Obligation. The people sit. When the Sermon is ended, the profession of faith is made, when prescribed. The people stand.

The Creed

Credo in unum Deum, Patrem omnipoténtem, factórem cæli et terræ, visibílium ómnium et invisibílium. Et in unum Dóminum Jesum Christum, Fílium	**We believe in one God, the Father, the Almighty, maker of heaven and earth, of all that is, seen and unseen. We believe in one Lord, Jesus Christ,**

Dei unigénitum, et ex Patre natum ante ómnia sǽcula. Deum de Deo, lumen de lúmine, Deum verum de Deo vero, génitum, non factum, consubstantiálem Patri: per quem ómnia facta sunt. Qui propter nos hómines et propter nostram salútem descéndit de cælis. *(All bow.)* Et incarnátus est de Spiritu Sancto ex María Vírgine, et homo factus est. Crucifíxus étiam pro nobis sub Póntio Piláto; passus et sepúltus est, et resurréxit tértia die, secúndum Scriptúras, et ascéndit in cælum, sedet ad déxteram Patris. Et íterum ventúrus est cum glória, judicáre vivos et mórtuos, cujus regni non erit finis.

the only Son of God, eternally begotten of the Father, God from God, Light from Light, true God from true God, begotten, not made, of one Being with the Father. Through him all things were made. For us men and for our salvation he came down from heaven: (all bow) by the power of the Holy Spirit he became incarnate from the Virgin Mary, and was made man. For our sake he was crucified under Pontius Pilate; he suffered death and was buried. On the third day he rose again in accordance with the Scriptures; he ascended into heaven and is seated at the right hand of the Father. He will come again in glory to judge the living and the dead, and his kingdom will have no

Et in Spiritum Sanctum, Dóminum et vivificántem: qui ex Patre Filióque procédit. Qui cum Patre et Fílio simul adorátur et conglorificátur: qui locútus est per prophétas. Et unam, sanctam, cathólicam et apostólicam Ecclésiam. Confiteor unum baptísma in remissiónem peccatórum. Et exspécto resurrectiónem mortuórum, et vitam ventúri sáeculi. Amen.

end. We believe in the Holy Spirit, the Lord, the giver of life, who proceeds from the Father and the Son. With the Father and the Son he is worshipped and glorified. He has spoken through the Prophets. We believe in one holy catholic and apostolic Church. We acknowledge one baptism for the forgiveness of sins. We look for the resurrection of the dead, and the life of the world to come. Amen.

The Prayer of the Faithful

The Bidding Prayer, which may now follow, is preceded by the Invitation and consists of a series of Petitions, each of which ends: Lord hear us. The people answer:
R. Lord graciously hear us.

The final Petition is: Let us commend ourselves and all God's people, living and dead, to the intercession of our Blessed Lady, the glorious and ever-virgin Mother of God. *The people may then recite the Hail Mary, after which there is a pause for silent prayer. At the end of the Prayer, which follows, the people answer:* **Amen**

The Liturgy
‎£ OF THE Eucharist ‎£

The Offertory

The Offertory Antiphon or a Hymn may be sung while the bread and wine are brought to the altar. The people sit. The priest, standing at the altar, takes the paten with the bread and, holding it slightly raised above the altar says:

Pr. Blessed are you, Lord, God of all creation.
Through your goodness we have this bread to offer,
which earth has given and human hands have made.
It will become for us the bread of life.
R. Blessed be God for ever.
(If singing is in progress, this response is omitted).

The priest pours wine and a little water into the chalice, saying in a low voice:

Pr. By the mystery of this water and wine may we
come to share in the divinity of Christ,
who humbled himself to share in our humanity.

Then he takes the chalice and raises it a little above the altar, saying:

Pr. Blessed are you, Lord, God of all creation. Through your goodness we have this wine to offer, fruit of the vine and work of human hands. It will become our spiritual drink.
R. Blessed be God for ever.
(If singing is in progress, this response is omitted).

The Liturgy of the Eucharist

The priest bows and says silently:
Pr. Lord God, we ask you to receive us and be pleased with the sacrifice we offer you with humble and contrite hearts.

The priest then washes his hands at the side of the altar, saying in a low voice:
Pr. Lord, wash away my iniquity; cleanse me from my sin.

The people stand. At the centre of the altar, facing the people, the priest says:
Pr. Pray, brethren, that my sacrifice and yours may be acceptable to God, the almighty Father.
R. May the Lord accept the sacrifice at your hands for the praise and glory of his name, for our good, and the good of all his Church.

The priest then recites the Prayer over the Gifts. At the end of the Prayer:
R. Amen.

The Eucharistic Prayer

The priest begins:
Pr. The Lord be with you.
R. And also with you.
Pr. Lift up your hearts.
R. We lift them up to the Lord.

Pr. Let us give thanks to the Lord our God.
R. It is right to give him thanks and praise.

The priest then reads the Preface, which varies according to the Season or the Feast. Then all join with the priest saying:

Sanctus, Sanctus, Sanctus, Dóminus Deus Sábaoth. Pleni sunt cæli et terra glória tua. Hosánna in excélsis. Benedictus qui venit in nómine Dómini. Hosánna in excelsis.	**Holy, holy, holy Lord, God of power and might, heaven and earth are full of your glory. Hosanna in the highest. Blessed is he who comes in the name of the Lord. Hosanna in the highest.**

Then follows one of the Eucharistic Prayers.

Eucharistic Prayer I

The celebrant sings or says:

Pr. We come to you, Father, with praise and thanksgiving, through Jesus Christ your Son. Through him we ask you to accept and bless these gifts we offer you in sacrifice. We offer them for your holy catholic Church, watch over it, Lord, and guide it; grant it peace and unity throughout the world. We offer them for *N.* our Pope, for *N.* our bishop, and for all who hold and teach the catholic faith that comes to us from the apostles. Remember,

The Liturgy of the Eucharist

Lord, your people, especially those for whom we now pray, *N*. and *N*. *(Pray silently for the living).*

Remember all of us gathered here before you. You know how firmly we believe in you and dedicate ourselves to you. We offer you this sacrifice of praise for ourselves and those who are dear to us. We pray to you, our living and true God, for our well-being and redemption. In union with the whole Church we honour Mary, the ever-virgin mother of Jesus Christ our Lord and God. We honour Joseph, her husband, the apostles and martyrs Peter and Paul, Andrew, James, John, Thomas, James, Philip, Bartholomew, Matthew, Simon and Jude; we honour Linus, Cletus, Clement, Sixtus, Cornelius, Cyprian, Lawrence, Chrysogonus, John and Paul, Cosmas and Damian and all the saints. May their merits and prayers gain us your constant help and protection. Through Christ our Lord. Amen.

Father, accept this offering from your whole family. Grant us your peace in this life, save us from final damnation, and count us among those you have chosen. Through Christ our Lord. Amen.

Bless and approve our offering; make it acceptable to you, an offering in spirit and in truth. Let it become for us the body and blood of Jesus Christ, your only Son, our Lord. The day before he suffered he took bread in his sacred hands and looking up to heaven, to you, his almighty

Father, he gave you thanks and praise. He broke the bread, gave it to his disciples, and said:

'Take this, all of you and eat it: this is my body which will be given up for you.'

When supper was ended, he took the cup. Again he gave you thanks and praise, gave the cup to his disciples, and said:

'Take this, all of you, and drink from it: this is the cup of my blood, the blood of the new and everlasting covenant. It will be shed for you and for all so that sins may be forgiven. Do this in memory of me.'

The celebrant invites us as follows:
   Pr. Let us proclaim the mystery of faith:

The people acclaim using one of the following:
1. Christ has died, Christ is risen, Christ will come again.

---

2. Dying you destroyed our death, rising you restored our life. Lord Jesus, come in glory.

---

3. When we eat this bread and drink this cup, we proclaim your death, Lord Jesus, until you come in glory.

---

4. Lord, by your cross and resurrection you have set us free. You are the Saviour of the world.

The Liturgy of the Eucharist

(*For Ireland only:* **My Lord and my God.**)

Pr. Father, we celebrate the memory of Christ, your Son. We, your people and your ministers, recall his passion, his resurrection from the dead, and his ascension in glory; and from the many gifts you have given us we offer to you, God of glory and majesty, this holy and perfect sacrifice: the bread of life and the cup of eternal salvation.

Look with favour on these offerings and accept them as once you accepted the gifts of your servant Abel, the sacrifice of Abraham, our Father in faith, and the bread and wine offered by your priest Melchizedek.

Almighty God, we pray that your angel may take this sacrifice to your altar in heaven. Then, as we receive from this altar the sacred body and blood of your Son, let us be filled with every grace and blessing. Through Christ our Lord. Amen.

Remember, Lord, those who have died and have gone before us marked with the sign of faith, especially those for whom we now pray, *N.* and *N.* (*Pray silently for the dead*).

May these, and all who sleep in Christ, find in your presence light, happiness, and peace. Through Christ our Lord. Amen.

For ourselves, too, we ask some share in the fellowship of your apostles and martyrs, with John the Baptist, Stephen, Matthias, Barnabas, Ignatius, Alexander, Marcellinus, Peter, Felicity, Perpetua, Agatha, Lucy, Agnes, Cecilia, Anastasia and all the saints.

Though we are sinners, we trust in your mercy and love. Do not consider what we truly deserve, but grant us your forgiveness.

Through Christ our Lord you give us all these gifts. You fill them with life and goodness, you bless them and make them holy.

Through him, with him, in him, in the unity of the Holy Spirit, all glory and honour is yours, almighty Father, for ever and ever. **R. Amen.**

For the Communion Rite turn to page 81.

Eucharistic Prayer II

The celebrant sings or says:
Pr. Lord, you are holy indeed, the fountain of all holiness. Let your Spirit come upon these gifts to make them holy, so that they may become for us the body and blood of our Lord, Jesus Christ.

Before he was given up to death, a death he freely accepted, he took bread and gave you thanks. He broke the bread, gave it to his disciples, and said:

'Take this, all of you and eat it: this is my body which will be given up for you.'

When supper was ended, he took the cup. Again he gave you thanks and praise, gave the cup to his disciples, and said:

THE LITURGY OF THE EUCHARIST

'Take this, all of you, and drink from it: this is the cup of my blood, the blood of the new and everlasting covenant. It will be shed for you and for all so that sins may be forgiven. Do this in memory of me.'

The celebrant invites us as follows:
Pr. Let us proclaim the mystery of faith:

The people respond as on page 72.

Pr. In memory of his death and resurrection, we offer you, Father, this life-giving bread, this saving cup. We thank you for counting us worthy to stand in your presence and serve you. May all of us who share in the body and blood of Christ be brought together in unity by the Holy Spirit.

Lord, remember your Church throughout the world; make us grow in love, together with *N.* our Pope, *N.* our bishop, and all the clergy.

In Masses for the Dead these words may be added:
Remember *N.* whom you have called from this life. In baptism he/she died with Christ: may he/she also share his resurrection.

Remember our brothers and sisters who have gone to their rest in the hope of rising again; bring them and all the departed into the light of your presence. Have mercy on us all; make us worthy to share eternal life with Mary, the virgin mother of God, with the apostles, and with all the saints who have done your will throughout the ages. May we praise you in union with them, and give you glory through your Son, Jesus Christ.

Through him, with him, in him, in the unity of the Holy Spirit, all glory and honour is yours, almighty Father, for ever and ever. **R. Amen.**

For the Communion Rite turn to page 81.

Eucharistic Prayer III

The celebrant sings or says:
Pr. Father, you are holy indeed, and all creation rightly gives you praise. All life, all holiness comes from you through your Son, Jesus Christ our Lord, by the working of the Holy Spirit. From age to age you gather a people to yourself, so that from east to west a perfect offering may be made to the glory of your name. And so, Father, we bring you these gifts. We ask you to make them holy by the power of your Spirit, that they may become the body and blood of your Son, our Lord Jesus Christ, at whose command we celebrate this Eucharist.

On the night he was betrayed, he took bread and gave you thanks and praise. He broke the bread, gave it to his disciples, and said:

The Liturgy of the Eucharist

'Take this, all of you and eat it: this is my body which will be given up for you.'

When supper was ended, he took the cup. Again he gave you thanks and praise, gave the cup to his disciples, and said:

'Take this, all of you, and drink from it: this is the cup of my blood, the blood of the new and everlasting covenant. It will be shed for you and for all so that sins may be forgiven. Do this in memory of me.'

The celebrant invites us as follows:
Pr. Let us proclaim the mystery of faith:

The people respond as on page 72.
Pr. Father, calling to mind the death your Son endured for our salvation, his glorious resurrection and ascension into heaven, and ready to greet him when he comes again, we offer you in thanksgiving his holy and living sacrifice. Look with favour on your Church's offering, and see the Victim whose death has reconciled us to yourself. Grant that we, who are nourished by his body and blood, may be filled with his Holy Spirit, and become one body, one spirit in Christ.

May he makes us an everlasting gift to you and enable us to share in the inheritance of your saints, with Mary, the virgin mother of God; with the apostles, the martyrs, Saint *N. (the saint of the day or the patron saint)* and all your saints, on whose constant intercession we rely for help.

Lord, may this sacrifice, which has made our peace with you, advance the peace and salvation of all the world. Strengthen in faith and love your pilgrim Church on earth; your servant, Pope *N.*, our bishop *N.* and all the bishops, with the clergy and the entire people your Son has gained for you. Father, hear the prayers of the family you have gathered here before you. In mercy and love unite all your children wherever they may be.

Welcome into your kingdom our departed brothers and sisters, and all who have left this world in your friendship. We hope to enjoy for ever the vision of your glory, through Christ our Lord, from whom all good things come.

Or, in Masses for the Dead:
Remember *N.* In baptism he/she died with Christ: may he/she also share his resurrection, when Christ will raise our mortal bodies and make them like his own in glory. Welcome into your kingdom our departed brothers and sisters, and all who have left this world in your friendship. There we hope to share in your glory when every tear will be wiped away. On that day we shall see you, our God, as you are. We shall become like you and praise you for ever through Christ our Lord, from whom all good things come.

Through him, with him, in him, in the unity of the Holy Spirit, all glory and honour is yours almighty Father, for ever and ever. **R. Amen.**

For the Communion Rite turn to page 81.

The Liturgy of the Eucharist

Eucharistic Prayer IV

The celebrant sings or says:

Pr. Father, we acknowledge your greatness: all your actions show your wisdom and love. You formed man in your own likeness and set him over the whole world to serve you, his creator, and to rule over all creatures. Even when he disobeyed you and lost your friendship you did not abandon him to the power of death, but helped all men to seek and find you. Again and again you offered a covenant to man, and through the prophets taught him to hope for salvation. Father, you so loved the world that in the fullness of time you sent your only Son to be our Saviour. He was conceived through the power of the Holy Spirit, and born of the Virgin Mary, a man like us in all things but sin. To the poor he proclaimed the good news of salvation, to prisoners, freedom, and to those in sorrow, joy. In fulfilment of your will he gave himself up to death; but by rising from the dead, he destroyed death and restored life. And that we might live no longer for ourselves but for him, he sent the Holy Spirit from you, Father, as his first gift to those who believe, to complete his work on earth and bring us the fullness of grace.

Father, may this Holy Spirit sanctify these offerings. Let them become the body and blood of Jesus Christ our Lord as we celebrate the great mystery which he left us as an everlasting covenant. He always loved those who were his own in the world. When the time came for him to be glorified by you, his heavenly Father, he showed the depth of his love. While they were at supper, he took bread, said the blessing, broke the bread and gave it to his disciples, saying:

'Take this, all of you and eat it: this is my body which will be given up for you.'

In the same way, he took the cup, filled with wine. He gave you thanks, and giving the cup to his disciples, said:

'Take this, all of you, and drink from it: this is the cup of my blood, the blood of the new and everlasting covenant. It will be shed for you and for all so that sins may be forgiven. Do this in memory of me.'

The celebrant invites us as follows:
Pr. Let us proclaim the mystery of faith:

The people respond as on page 72.
Pr. Father, we now celebrate this memorial of our redemption. We recall Christ's death, his descent among the dead, his resurrection, and his ascension to your right hand; and, looking forward to his coming in glory, we offer you his body and blood, the acceptable sacrifice, which brings salvation to the whole world. Lord, look upon this sacrifice which you have given to your Church; and by your Holy Spirit, gather all who share this one bread and one cup into the body of Christ, a living sacrifice of praise.

Lord, remember those for whom we offer this sacrifice, especially N. our Pope, N. our bishop, and bishops and clergy everywhere. Remember those who take part in this offering, those here present and all your people, and all who seek you with a sincere heart. Remember those who have died in the peace of Christ and all the dead whose faith is known to you alone. Father, in your mercy grant also to us, your children, to enter into our heavenly inheritance in the company of the Virgin Mary the Mother of God, and your apostles and saints. Then, in your kingdom, freed from the corruption of sin and death, we shall sing your glory with every creature through Christ our Lord, through whom you give us everything that is good.

Through him, with him, in him, in the unity of the Holy Spirit, all glory and honour is yours, almighty Father, for ever and ever. **R. Amen.**

The Communion Rite

The people stand.

Præceptis salutáribus móniti, et divína institutióne formati, audémus dicere:	**Let us pray with confidence to the Father in the words our Saviour gave us:**

Priest and people continue:

Pater noster, qui es in cælis; sanctificétur nomen tuum; advéniat regnum tuum; fiat voluntas tua sicut in cælo, et in terra. Panem nostrum cotidiánum da nobis hódie; et dimítte nobis débita nostra, sicut et nos dimíttimus debitóribus nostris; et ne nos indúcas in tentatiónem; sed líbera nos a malo.

Our Father, who art in heaven, hallowed be thy name. Thy kingdom come. Thy will be done on earth, as it is in heaven. Give us this day our daily bread, and forgive us our trespasses, as we forgive those who trespass against us, and lead us not into temptation, but deliver us from evil.

The priest continues alone:
Pr. Deliver us, Lord, from every evil, and grant us peace in our day. In your mercy keep us free from sin and protect us from all anxiety as we wait in joyful hope for the coming of our Saviour, Jesus Christ.

The people acclaim:
R. For the kingdom, the power, and the glory are yours, now and for ever.

The priest continues alone:
Pr. Lord, Jesus Christ, you said to your apostles: I leave you peace, my peace I give you. Look not on our sins, but

The Liturgy of the Eucharist

on the faith of your Church, and grant us the peace and unity of your kingdom where you live for ever and ever.
R. Amen.
Pr. The peace of the Lord be with you always.
R. And also with you.

If the people are to exchange a sign of peace, according to local custom, the priest adds:
Pr. Let us offer each other the sign of peace.

The priest breaks the host over the paten and puts a small piece of it into the chalice, saying silently:
Pr. May this mingling of the Body and Blood of our Lord Jesus Christ bring eternal life to us who receive it.

While the host is being broken the people say:

Agnus Dei, qui tollis peccáta mundi: miserére nobis.	**Lamb of God, you take away the sins of the world: have mercy on us.**
Agnus Dei, qui tollis peccáta mundi: miserére nobis.	**Lamb of God, you take away the sins of the world: have mercy on us.**
Agnus Dei, qui tollis peccáta mundi: dona nobis pacem.	**Lamb of God, you take away the sins of the world: grant us peace.**

The people kneel. The priest says one of the following prayers in a low voice:
Pr. Lord Jesus Christ, Son of the living God, by the will of the Father and the work of the Holy Spirit your death brought life to the world. By your holy Body and Blood free me from all my sins and from every evil. Keep me faithful to your teaching, and never let me be parted from you.
Or:
Lord Jesus Christ, with faith in your love and mercy I eat your Body and drink your Blood. Let it not bring me condemnation, but health in mind and body.

The priest genuflects, takes the host and, holding it slightly raised above the paten, facing the people, says:
Pr. This is the Lamb of God who takes away the sins of the world. Happy are those who are called to his supper.

Then, together with the people, he says, once only:
R. Lord, I am not worthy to receive you, but only say the word and I shall be healed.

Before consuming the host, the priest says silently:
Pr. May the Body of Christ bring me to everlasting life.

The Communion Antiphon follows.
The priest goes to the communicants and says to each:
   Pr. The Body of Christ.
   R. Amen.

The Liturgy of the Eucharist

While cleansing the sacred vessels the priest says silently:
Pr. Lord, may I receive these gifts in purity of heart. May they bring me healing and strength, now and for ever.
Communion over, the priest may sit at the chair for a time, while all continue to make their thanksgiving in silence.

Then standing at the chair or at the altar the priest says:
    Pr. Let us pray.

Priest and people pray in silence for a while, unless the silence has already been observed. Then the priest says the Prayer after Communion for which the people stand.

At the end of the Prayer:
R. Amen.

The Concluding Rite

If there are any short announcements they are made now.
    Pr. The Lord be with you.
    R. And also with you.

The priest blesses the people with these words:
    Pr. May almighty God bless you, the Father, and the Son, ✠ and the Holy Spirit.
    R. Amen.

The priest dismisses the people with one of the following formulas:

1. Go in the peace of Christ.
Or:
2. The Mass is ended, go in peace.
Or:
3. Go in peace to love and serve the Lord.
R. Thanks be to God.

CTS
MEMBERSHIP

We hope you have enjoyed reading this booklet. If you would like to read more of our booklets or find out more about CTS - why not do one of the following?

1. Join our Readers CLUB.
We will send you a copy of every new booklet we publish, through the post to your address. You'll get 20% off the price too.

2. Support our work and Mission.
Become a CTS Member. Every penny you give will help spread the faith throughout the world. What's more, you'll be entitled to special offers exclusive to CTS Members.

3. Ask for our Information Pack.
Become part of the CTS Parish Network by selling CTS publications in your own parish.

Call us now on 020 7640 0042 or return this form to us at CTS, 40-46 Harleyford Road, London SE11 5AY
Fax: 020 7640 0046 email: info@cts-online.org.uk

❏ I would like to join the *CTS Readers Club*
❏ Please send me details of how to join CTS as a *Member*
❏ Please send me a *CTS Information Pack*

Name:..
Address:..
....
Post Code:..
Phone: ....
email address: ....

Registered charity no. 218951.
Registered in England as a company limited by guarantee no.57374.